MMS
Sample
Not For Sale

AF088949

By Shalini Vallepur

BookLife PUBLISHING

©2019
BookLife Publishing Ltd.
King's Lynn
Norfolk PE30 4LS

All rights reserved.
Printed in Malaysia.

A catalogue record for this book is available from the British Library.

ISBN: 978-1-78637-727-2

Written by:
Shalini Vallepur

Edited by:
John Wood

Designed by:
Dan Scase

All facts, statistics, web addresses and URLs in this book were verified as valid and accurate at time of writing. No responsibility for any changes to external websites or references can be accepted by either the author or publisher.

Photo Credits

All images are courtesy of Shutterstock.com, unless otherwise specified. With thanks to Getty Images, Thinkstock Photo and iStockphoto. Front Cover – Vitaly Korovin, thaikrit, M. Unal Ozmen, VectorPot, vimolsiri.s, Ku_suriuri, akepong srichaichana, Jane Kelly, Romariolen. 3 – M. Unal Ozmen, Ku_suriuri, akepong srichaichana, Romariolen. 4 – Monkey Business Images, MicroOne. 5 – Photographee. eu. 6 – Robert Kneschke, gpointstudio, Hung Chung Chih. 7 – A3pfamily. 8 – nehophoto, FARBAI. 9 – Billion Photos, timquo, Max Lashcheuski. 10 – Billion Photos, M. Unal Ozmen, timquo, Tim UR, Anton Starikov. 11 – Robert Kneschke. 12 – Maxx-Studio, Tatiana Volgutova. 13 – tinka's. 14 – Ahanov Michael, uiliaaa. 15 – Olga Dekush. 16 – Robyn Mackenzie, uiliaaa. 17 – Joellen L Armstrong, tetxu, SOMMAI, Robyn Mackenzie, Gita Kulinitch Studio, Moving Moment. 18 – beats1, Marnikus. 19 – CalypsoArt. 20 – Africa Studio, Ildi Papp, Anuchart Sungthong. 21 – Olly Molly, mything. 22 – R Kristoffersen, Irina Qiwi. 23 – KaliAntye, Studio 1One, Toey Toey. Chalk boards – SeDmi. Wood Background – primopiano. Plate – Vitaly Korovin. Notepad – style_TTT.

Contents

Page 4	**Diverse Diets**
Page 6	**What Is Diabetes?**
Page 8	**What Are Carbohydrates?**
Page 10	**Smart Swaps**
Page 12	**Brilliant Banana Ice Cream**
Page 16	**Smart Swaps**
Page 18	**Quick Quinoa Salad**
Page 22	**Living with Diabetes**
Page 24	**Glossary and Index**

Words that look like **this** can be found in the glossary on page 24.

Diverse Diets

There are lots of different foods all around the world. A person's diet is made up of the food that they normally eat every day. Diets can be **diverse**, as different people eat different foods.

What do you have for lunch at school?

We all make choices when it comes to our diets. Some people don't have a choice. A person might not be able to eat certain foods because they have a health <u>condition</u> such as diabetes.

What Is Diabetes?

Certain foods that we eat are turned into sugars. The sugars stay in our blood and a **hormone** called insulin tells our body to use the sugars for energy.

We need energy to do everything — even sleeping!

Diabetes affects insulin. If insulin does not work, sugars in the blood can't be used for energy. The sugars stay in the blood and make blood sugar levels high.

High blood sugar levels can make someone feel very tired and thirsty.

What Are Carbohydrates?

Bread, pasta, rice and cereal are known as starchy carbs.

A good diet can help control blood sugar levels. We get sugars from foods that are called carbohydrates, or carbs for short. When we eat carbs, they get broken down into sugar.

Simple Sugars

Sugar by itself is a carb called simple sugar. Foods that are made of sugar or have a lot of sugar added to them are not healthy carbs. They make blood sugar levels go high quickly.

CHOCOLATE CAKE

SWEETS

KETCHUP

Smart Swaps

Simple sugars are found in fruits and milk. This sugar is **natural** and there is not a lot of it. We can swap bad simple sugars for good ones.

Fruits are a good source of **vitamins** and **fibre**. They keep us healthy and make the perfect sweet snack. We can use fruits to make a healthy dessert…

Brilliant Banana Ice Cream

Ice cream sometimes has a lot of sugar added to it. Let's use bananas to make a super-simple ice cream.

Equipment you will need:

- Knife
- Freezer bags
- Blender

This recipe is so simple that it only needs one ingredient! This recipe is for two people.

Ingredients you will need:

- Six **ripe** bananas with brown spots

Let's Cook!

1. Chop the bananas into chunks that are around five centimetres in size.
2. Place the chunks into the freezer bags and pop them into the freezer.
3. Freeze for six hours.
4. Put the frozen banana chunks into a blender.
5. Blend until the bananas are smooth like ice cream.

Do you like nuts? You can sprinkle a few nuts on top for some added crunch. Or you could add some cinnamon to the mix for a new taste.

Smart Swaps

Brown rice, brown pasta and brown bread are all examples of wholegrain foods.

It is important for a person with diabetes to keep their blood sugar levels steady and not too high. Wholegrain carbs are good for this as they have a lot of fibre and raise blood sugar levels slowly.

Wholegrains are changed into refined grains to make foods such as white bread. The fibre is lost, which makes blood sugar levels rise quickly when eaten. Here are some food swaps:

Quick Quinoa Salad

Let's use quinoa to make a quick and healthy lunch.

Equipment you will need:

- Kitchen scales
- Measuring jug
- Sieve
- Saucepan
- Blender
- Big serving bowl
- Knife
- Tablespoon

Ingredients you will need for four people:

- 85 grams of raw quinoa
- One pepper chopped – any colour you like!
- Half a cucumber
- Two tomatoes chopped

RAW QUINOA

COOKED QUINOA

GARLIC CLOVES

To make the dressing:

- One tablespoon of olive oil
- Four tablespoons of rice vinegar
- Two cloves of garlic, chopped into very small pieces
- Pinch each of salt and pepper

Let's Cook!

1. Rinse the quinoa in the sieve under the tap for a minute.

2. Pour 375 millilitres of water into the saucepan and bring the water to the boil.

3. Add the quinoa to the water and bring it to the boil, then lower the heat to a **simmer** for 15 minutes.

4. Put the dressing ingredients into the blender and blend for a few seconds.

5. Put all the vegetables into your serving bowl.

6. When the quinoa has **absorbed** all the water, let it cool before adding it to the serving bowl.

7. Pour the dressing over everything in the serving bowl and **toss** the salad.

This tasty salad has lots of fibre so it will not raise blood sugar levels too quickly.

Living With Diabetes

It is important for a person with diabetes to keep track of their blood sugar levels. A finger-prick test is one way of checking how much sugar is in someone's blood.

Blood sugar levels fall after doing a lot of exercise.

Having diabetes does not mean that you will never eat a slice of cake again. Some sugary foods can be eaten from time to time as part of a healthy, balanced diet and active lifestyle.

Glossary

absorbed	to have taken in or soaked up
condition	an illness or other medical problem
diverse	different kinds of things
fibre	a part of some foods that takes longer for the human body to break down
hormone	a type of chemical in your body that tells cells what to do
natural	found in nature and not made by humans
ripe	when a fruit is ready to be eaten
simmer	when something is cooked on a low heat and not boiled
toss	to gently mix something
vitamins	things needed for normal and healthy growth

Index

bananas 12–15
blood 6–9, 16–17, 21–22
carbohydrates 8–9, 16
energy 6–7
diet 4–5, 8, 23
fruits 10–11
ingredients 13, 19, 21
insulin 6–7
lunch 4, 18
quinoa 17–21
sugar 6–10, 12, 16–17, 21–23
sweets 9–10
vegetables 21